YOU CAN DRAW

Baby Animals

Written by Debby Henwood

Willowisp Press®

Published by Willowisp Press, Inc.
401 E. Wilson Bridge Road, Worthington, Ohio 43085

Printed in the United States of America

10 9 8 7 6 5 4 3

ISBN 0-87406-270-5

You can learn to draw baby animals. Just follow the step-by-step instructions in this book. Draw the basic shapes. Then add shapes for the legs, feet, ears, and tail.

Improve the basic form until it is just the way you like it. This is the time to add detail and shading. Practice until you feel the drawing is just right.

BEFORE YOU BEGIN

Remember these drawing tips while you draw the baby animals shown in this book.

1. Use round, oval, and kidney shapes to draw the body parts of most animals. Draw the shapes lightly in pencil. Do not lift your pencil off the paper when drawing each shape.

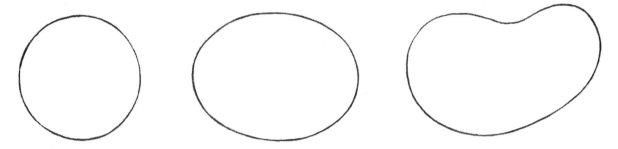

2. When the basic shapes are drawn, erase any guidelines you do not need. Then add final details.

3. Practice holding a pencil to make different shading strokes. Example number 1 shows how to make fine, short, zigzag strokes. The second example shows how to hold a pencil when drawing broad strokes. Use broad strokes to shade fur patterns and darkened areas of your drawing.

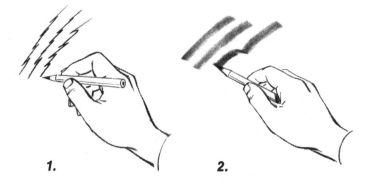

1.   *2.*

4. Shade darkened areas of the animals. Darken inside the ears, under the chin, and underneath the body.

5. Draw the animals walking, jumping, or standing. Practice drawing an animal in this book. Then try drawing the animal in a different position.

6. Add the background that is best for the animal. These details will finish off the drawing, giving it an extra-special look.

TIGER CUB

1. *Lightly draw a circle for the head. Then draw the eye line. Draw a kidney shape for the body.*

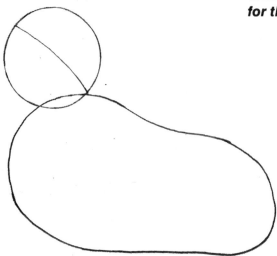

2. *Add lines for the muzzle and ear shapes. Use free-flowing lines for the legs and tail. Complete the basic drawing with neck lines. Begin to add detail to the face.*

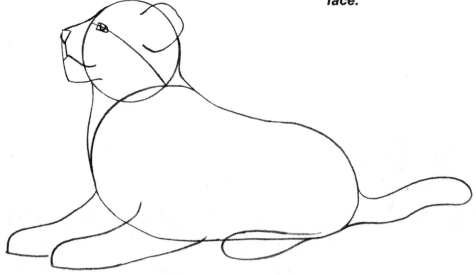

3. Draw a zigzag line around the basic shapes to look like fur. Erase the guide-lines. Use the side of your pencil lead to draw zigzag lines for the "stripes."

4. Add detail lines to the face, ears, and paws. Use light shading lines over the body to give the cub a finished look.

ELEPHANT CALF

1. Draw an oval for the body. Then use a free-flowing line for the head shape.

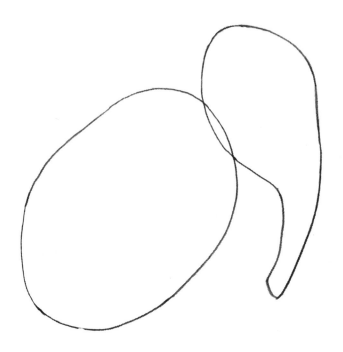

2. Draw a curved line for the ear. Draw a short line to show the ear that is mostly hidden. Draw an eye line. Add lines for the leg and tail shapes.

3. *Erase the guidelines. Use the side of your pencil lead to draw "wrinkles" on the body.*

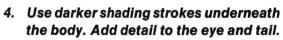

4. **Use darker shading strokes underneath the body. Add detail to the eye and tail.**

CHIMPANZEE

1. This chimp is swinging on a tree limb. Draw the head first. Then draw the body shapes. Add eye and nose lines to the head.

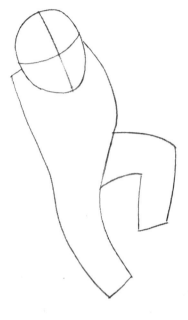

2. Use the guidelines on the head to add the face. Add the feet and ears.

3. Draw zigzag lines around the body shapes to show the fur. Erase the guidelines. Add fur lines to the face. Begin to add shading.

4. Follow the example to draw more shading strokes. Finish the face. Add a tree limb.

LAMB

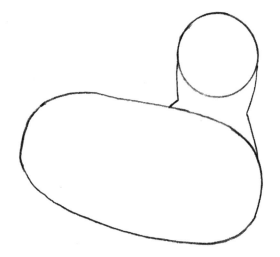

1. Draw the head and body shapes. Connect the shapes with neck lines.

2. Add free-flowing lines for the legs, ears, and hooves. Draw eye and nose lines. Add a shape for the muzzle.

3. **Draw soft curly lines around the outside of the shapes. Add detail to the face. Put a bell on the lamb.**

4. **Erase the guidelines. Use dark shading strokes underneath the body. Use shading around the face.**

FOAL

1. *Draw the head and body shapes. Connect them with curved neck lines.*

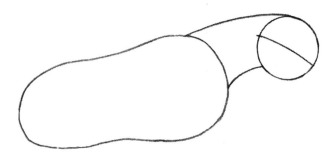

2. *Use free-flowing lines for the legs. Add shapes for the muzzle and ears. Draw an eye line.*

3. Add detail to the face and nose. Add the flowing mane and tail.

4. Erase the guidelines. Use shading strokes to show the muscle tone on the foal.

KITTEN

1. Draw the body shapes.

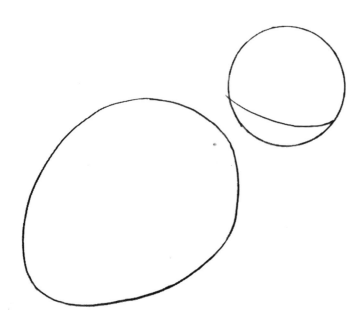

**2. Connect the shapes with the neck lines.
Add leg, muzzle, and ear shapes.**

3. **Begin to add detail to the face. Draw zigzag lines around the body.**

4. **Erase the guidelines. Use light, thin lines for the fur over all the body. Then use dark shading strokes for the striped pattern. Add whiskers. Show a spool of thread.**

PUPPY

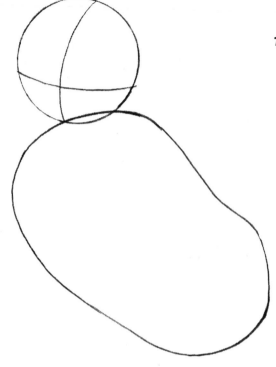

1. *Draw the basic body shapes. Add eye and nose lines.*

2. *Add shapes for the legs, tail, and floppy ears. Add the muzzle.*

3. **Draw shapes for the eyes. Add detail to the nose and paws. Draw zigzag lines for the fur.**

4. **Darken the eyes and nose. Use shading strokes to show the direction the fur grows. Add whiskers.**

PIGLET

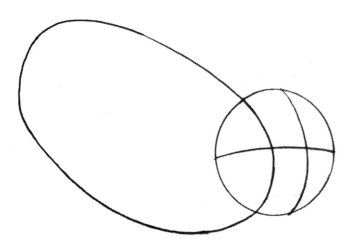

1. Draw a circle for the head. Then draw an oval for the body. Add eye and nose lines.

2. Add shapes for the legs, ears, nose, and chin.

3. **Begin to add detail to the face, nose, ears, and hooves. Add a tail. Draw zig-zag lines around the body shapes.**

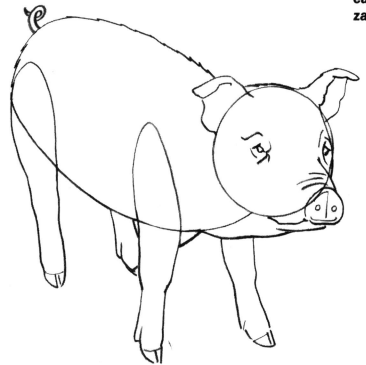

4. **Erase the guidelines. Shade inside the ears and under the chin. Add more shading to the body.**

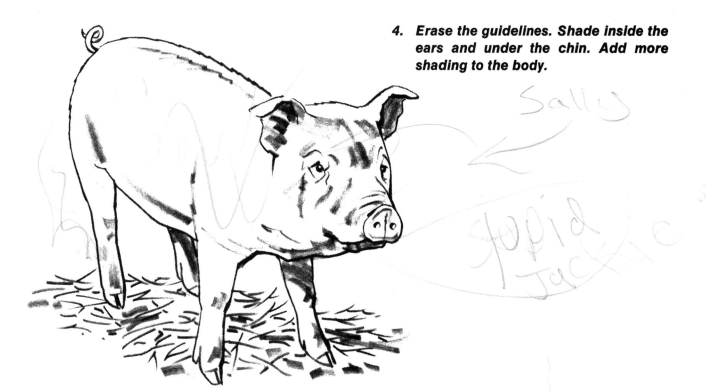

CALF

1. *Imagine the calf's body as a rectangle and a circle. Draw the basic shapes.*

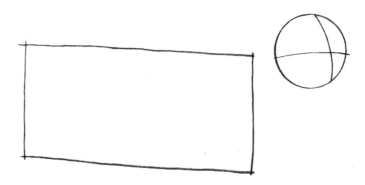

2. *Connect the shapes with neck lines. Add shapes for the legs, nose, and ears. Begin to show the tail along the rear leg.*

3. **Add detail to the eyes, ears, nose, and hooves.**

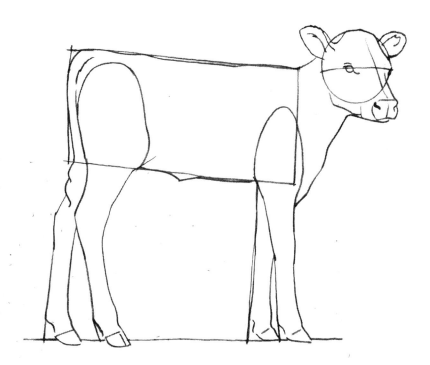

4. **Erase the guidelines. Finish the detail to the face and tail. Add shading.**

Margot

BEAR CUB

1. Draw the basic shapes. Connect with neck lines.

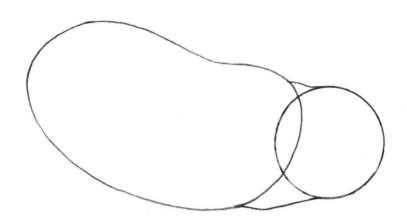

2. Add shapes for the muzzle, ears, legs, and paws.

3. **Draw a zigzag line around the outline of the body. Add detail to the eyes and nose. Use shading strokes to show the long fur on the neck and face. Add claws.**

4. **The fur lines are drawn starting from the back, and going down to the legs. Use quick, straight strokes. Add darkened areas.**

FAWN

1. *Draw and connect the basic shapes. Add the eye and nose lines.*

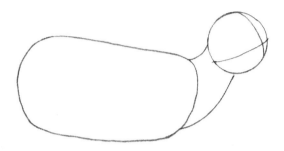

2. *Add shapes for the legs, ears, and muzzle.*

3. *Add detail to the face and hooves. Use zigzag lines to show fur. Draw a tail. Young deer have spots. Draw them.*

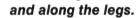

4. *Erase the guidelines. Add shading detail to the face, on the body, and along the legs.*

RACCOON KIT

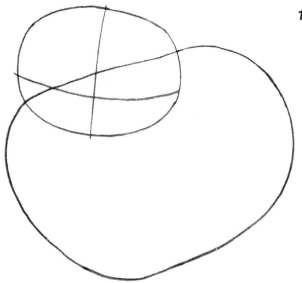

1. Draw the head, then the body shape.

2. Add shapes for the legs and tail. Add the ears and nose.

3. Draw a zigzag line around the outline. Draw the paws. Add the eyes. Draw a "mask" outline on the face. Fill in the mask with dark shading strokes. Use dark zigzag strokes for the rings on the tail.

4. Erase the guidelines. Draw light shading strokes for the fur on the body. Add darkened areas.

BEAVER KIT

1. Draw the basic shapes and the eye line.

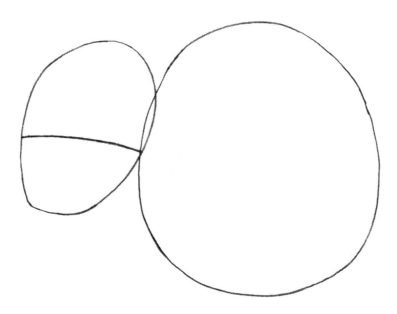

2. Add the zigzag outline. Add paws and a tail shape. Add shapes for the nose, eyes, and ear.

3. *Erase the guidelines. Add detail. Do light shading. Draw an apple.*

4. *Shade darkened areas.*

BUNNY

1. *Draw the basic body shapes.*

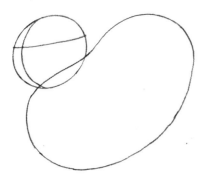

2. *Add shapes for the legs, ears, nose, and tail.*

3. *Draw a furry outline around the body shapes. Draw the eye and nose.*

4. *Erase the guidelines. Use thin shading strokes for the fur. Darken the fur tips. Leave the chest, tummy, and tail white. Add whiskers.*